My First
Horse and Pony Care
Book

KINGFISHER
LONDON & NEW YORK

Copyright © Macmillan Publishers International Ltd 2006, 2023
Published in the United States by Kingfisher
120 Broadway, New York, NY 10271
Kingfisher is a division of Macmillan Children's Books, London
ISBN 978-0-7534-7933-9

Distributed in the U.S. and Canada by Macmillan, 120 Broadway, New York, NY 10271

EU representative: Macmillan Publishers Ireland Ltd, 1st Floor, The Liffey Trust Centre, 117-126 Sheriff Street Upper, Dublin 1, D01 YC43.

Kingfisher books are available for special promotions and premiums. For details contact: Special Markets Department, Macmillan, 120 Broadway, New York, NY 10271. For more information, please visit www.kingfisherbooks.com.

Printed in China
10 9 8 7 6 5 4 3 2 1
1TR/0323/WKT/UG/128MA

library of congress cataloging-in-publication data
Draper, Judith.
  My first horse and pony care book/Judith Draper.—1st ed.
     p. cm.
  Includes bibliographical references and index.
  ISBN-13: 978-0-7534-5989-8 (alk. paper)
  ISBN-10: 0-7534-5989-2 (alk. paper)
  1. Horses—Juvenile literature. 2. Ponies—Juvenile literature. 3. Horsemanship—Juvenile literature. I. Title.
  SF302.D73 2006
  636.1'083--dc22
2006005962

Consultant: Elwyn Hartley Edwards
U.S. consultant: Lesley Ward
Editor: Russell Mclean
Coordinating editor: Stephanie Pliakas
Designers: Poppy Jenkins, Jack Clucas
Photographer: Matthew Roberts
Picture research manager: Cee Weston-Baker
Senior production controller: Lindsey Scott
DTP coordinator: Catherine Hibbert

Ponies supplied and produced by Justine Armstrong-Small BHSAI, pictured with Zin Zan (Champion Working Hunter, Horse of the Year Show 2004; Champion Lightweight Working Hunter, Royal Windsor Horse Show 2005)

Clothing and equipment supplied by Cuddly Ponies, Dublin Clothing, and Roma (www.dublinclothing.com).

MIX
Paper | Supporting responsible forestry
FSC
www.fsc.org   FSC® C116313

My First
Horse and Pony Care Book

Judith Draper

KINGFISHER
LONDON & NEW YORK

Contents

You and your horse

Having a horse or pony of your own is a lot of fun. If there is space to keep it at home, you can spend lots of time together and will quickly become friends. Horses need a lot of care, every day of the year, so you will need the help of an adult.

It is important to know how to handle horses confidently. Learn how to do this at a riding school or lesson barn before you have a horse or pony of your own.

Perfect partners

Your horse or pony should be the right size for you, not too big or too small. If you are a beginner, look for an older animal that is well trained and behaved.

You do not have to own a horse to become a good rider. Riding many different horses at a school is a good way to get better.

If you don't have a stable and pasture, you can keep your horse at someone else's stable. This is called a boarding barn.

Breeds

Many different breeds make good riding horses. They come in all types of shapes and sizes, from the little Welsh Mountain Pony to the Connemara, which is strong enough to carry a grown-up.

Connemara

The beautiful Connemara comes from Ireland. It jumps well and is a wonderful pony for shows and competitions.

The Caspian pony is the oldest breed of horse or pony. It stands no more than 12 hands high but is strong enough to be ridden by children.

The American Quarter Horse is one of the most popular breeds in the U.S. It is fast, reliable, and has an easygoing nature.

Welsh Section B

The Welsh Pony, known as Section B, is related to the tough Welsh Mountain Pony. It is bigger than its cousin and makes a perfect riding pony.

Shetland ponies are small and highly intelligent. They range from 7 to 11 hands in height, but are strong enough to be ridden by children.

Safety first!
For young riders, a horse or pony must have a kind nature and be easy to handle.

Grass and hay

A horse has a small stomach that cannot handle large meals. To stay healthy, it needs to eat small amounts of foods called roughage throughout the day. Grass and hay are types of roughage.

Tasty foods

A horse can spend up to 20 hours per day moving from place to place in search of the tastiest grasses and herbs. There is more nutrition in grasses in the spring and summer than in the fall and winter.

Safety first!

If a horse eats too much grass in the spring, it may get a painful disease called laminitis. This can damage the bones in its feet.

A horse eats more slowly if you feed it from a haynet. This is good for its stomach and stops it from getting bored.

Tie the haynet quite high up the stable wall so that your horse or pony cannot get its foot stuck in it.

Hay

Hay is made from specially grown long grasses that are cut from fields in the summer. The cut grasses are dried out and then made into bundles called bales. Hay provides roughage for stabled horses. It is also used for horses and ponies that live outside during the winter, when there is not much nutrition in grass.

TOP TIP

Soaking

If dusty hay makes your horse cough, soak the hay in water (for no more than 30 minutes) before feeding.

Feed bowls and water buckets should be kept clean. Scrub them regularly with freshwater.

Mix and measure

Write down all of the ingredients in your horse's feed and how much it has eaten at each meal. Measure its food carefully and mix the food up well.

sugar beet

feed scoop

Concentrated feed

When horses are ridden every day, they usually need extra food, called concentrated feed, to give them more energy. Horse pellets, sweet feed, oats, barley, corn, and sugar beets are all types of concentrated feed.

Sliced apples and carrots taste good and contain vitamins and minerals. They are called succulents.

Safe bucket

Stand your horse's water bucket inside an old rubber tire to stop it from knocking the bucket over.

Clean water

Horses and ponies must always have a supply of freshwater. In the stable, water can be given in a bucket. Check the bucket often to see if it needs to be refilled. In the field, use a special trough or a large plastic container.

Water buckets are usually made of plastic or rubber.

Cool down

Never give your horse or pony a long, cold drink right after riding it. This could cause an illness called colic. Walk it around until it is cool and has stopped breathing so hard.

Clean feet

Remember to pick out your horse's feet before you lead it out of the stable. This helps keep the yard clean.

Except in very bad weather, the top half of a stable door is left open to give your horse plenty of fresh air.

Always walk in the yard. Never run about.

American barn stables are found in many countries. They are very useful when the weather is bad.

Stables

There are two main types of stables. Outdoor stables are built in a row or around an open space called the stable yard. Stables can also be inside a much larger building. This is known as the American barn system.

When you walk through a door with your horse, lead it in a straight line so that it does not hurt itself.

A stable yard can get messy very quickly! Everyone needs to help keep it neat and tidy.

Light switches are placed where a horse cannot reach them with his teeth.

Drains have strong metal covers. They are kept clean all year round.

Stable doors have two bolts – one at the top and another at the bottom.

Stable windows are made of extra strong glass. Metal bars protect the glass.

Mucking out

If your horse is stabled, muck out its bed every day. Take manure and wet bedding to the muck pile. If your horse is left standing on dirty bedding, it could get an infection on its feet called thrush.

1 Use a pitchfork or shovel to pick up all of the manure and place it in a wheelbarrow.

2 Fork all of the dry bedding against the stable walls or, even better, into a clean corner.

3 Sweep the floor clean of any more manure and damp straw. Add these to the wheelbarrow.

4 Pile up fresh straw against the stable walls and cover it with some of the old straw. Use the rest to make a deep bed in the middle of the stable.

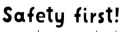

⚠️ Safety first!
After you have mucked out, never leave tools, such as pitchforks and shovels, in the stable in case your horse hurts itself.

Skipping out

Remove manure from your horse's bed as often as possible during the day. Use a pitchfork or a shovel and a container called a skip. Clearing away manure regularly helps keep the horse clean and makes mucking out in the morning easier.

Safety first!
If your horse is in the stable when you are mucking out or using a skip, always tie it up.

1 When you skip out a wood-shaving bed, use a special pitchfork to lift the manure into the skip.

2 Use the pitchfork to shake up and level off the bed. Make sure that the whole floor is covered with bedding.

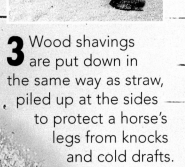

3 Wood shavings are put down in the same way as straw, piled up at the sides to protect a horse's legs from knocks and cold drafts.

A wood-shaving bed

Wood shavings make good stable bedding for horses and ponies that are allergic to straw or that tend to eat it and then become fat.

Handling a pony

It is very important to handle a horse or pony correctly and safely. You must learn how to ask it to move around in its stable, how to pick up its feet for cleaning, and how to lead it.

TOP TIP

Mounting

A well-trained horse should stand still while you mount. If your horse fidgets, someone must stand near its head.

It is common to lead a horse from the left side. But practice leading from the right, too, in case you ever need to.

Safety first!

Before leading your horse, run the stirrup irons up the leathers to stop them from flapping and scaring it.

Hold both reins in your right hand, just below the horse's head. Hold the buckle end of the reins with your left hand so that neither you nor the horse can trip over them.

The metal tying-up ring is attached tightly to the wall. A loop of baler twine or string is tied to it.

To stop your horse from undoing the knot with its teeth, pass the end of the lead rope through the loop.

TOP TIP

Safe string

Tie the rope to the string, not the ring. If the horse moves suddenly, the string will break and stop it from panicking.

In the stable

Tie up your horse whenever you are working in its stable—mucking out, grooming, or tacking up, for example. Ask an adult to show you how to tie a quick-release knot in the lead rope.

In the field

Horses and ponies are happiest when they are turned out in a field for at least part of the day. This is more natural than living in a stable. In the winter, your horse or pony may need to wear a turnout blanket to keep it warm and dry.

A sturdy run-in shed will give your horse a place where it can escape from very wet or very hot weather.

helmet

halter

lead rope

gloves

Putting a horse out in a field is called turning out. Your horse may get excited when it sees its friends, so keep it firmly under control.

Field visits

If you can, visit your horse or pony twice each day to check for any problems such as an injury or a blanket that has slipped.

Yew is very poisonous to horses and ponies. It must be dug or pulled out and then burned by an adult.

Your horse's field needs a supply of freshwater. A trough linked to a water pipe is best.

To help your horse avoid getting parasites, remove manure in a skip or wheelbarrow as often as you can.

**waterproof
turnout blanket**

TOP TIP

Locked up
Fences, gates, and locks should be checked often to make sure that they are secure and that your horse cannot get out.

Clean and neat

Grooming keeps a horse's skin clean and healthy by removing dried sweat and loose hair. It also makes it look neat. Groom a stabled horse every day, but groom a horse that lives in a field less because the grease and dirt in its coat will help keep it dry and warm.

1 Carefully remove patches of dirt and sweat with a dandy brush. Never use this stiff brush on your horse's head or belly.

In cold weather, keep your horse warm by covering half of it with a blanket while you groom the other half.

2 Use a soft body brush to groom the whole horse. Start just behind its ears and work toward its tail. Clean the bristles on a metal currycomb.

3 Use a soft body brush to groom the whole horse. Start just behind its ears and work toward its tail. Clean the bristles on a metal currycomb.

4 When you brush your horse's tail, stand to the side of it, not right behind, in case it kicks out.

body brush

Train a messy mane to lie on the correct side of the neck by wetting it and putting it into loose braids.

Safety first!
Before you start to groom, always tie up your horse with a halter and a rope.

Clean out the hooves with a hoof pick.

strong step

5 Finally, brush its head with a body brush. Be gentle and keep the bristles away from its eyes.

TOP TIP

Face sponge

Wipe around a horse's eyes and nose with a damp sponge. Use a different sponge to clean underneath the tail.

Manes and tails

A tidy mane and tail make a pony look extra smart. This is important for a show. A neat mane is easier to plait than a bushy, untidy one. It is easy to spoil a mane by not pulling it correctly, so this job should be done by an older person.

This rider is using a mane comb to comb back a section of hair. Then she pulls out the hairs that are left in the fingers of her other hand.

Pulling the mane

A pony's mane is thinned and shortened by pulling out some of the hair from the underneath, using the fingers and a metal mane-pulling comb.

This finished mane has been dampened with a water-brush to help the hairs lie flat.

The pony's tail is held away from his body when it is trimmed. This is the position that he carries it in when he is on the move.

hock

fetlock

Trimming the tail

Most ponies look best with their tails cut neatly to make a level, straight edge. The tail should hang between their hocks and their fetlocks. A very long tail will become muddy in winter.

TOP
TIP

Levelling

Round-ended scissors are always used to level off the ends of the pony's tail hairs.

Clipping

Most horses and ponies grow a thick coat in the winter, but this makes them sweaty and uncomfortable when they work. This is why a working horse or pony usually has part of its coat clipped by an experienced adult.

The person who clips the horse should wear a helmet.

Clipping a horse alone is difficult and even dangerous. A helper must always be present in order to keep the horse calm and to call for help if there is an accident.

A horse that is doing medium work has a "trace clip." Hair is clipped from part of its body and the underside of its neck.

A stabled horse that is doing medium to hard work has a "blanket clip." The hair is removed from part of its body and all of its neck.

The clippers are used in the opposite direction to the way that the horse's coat lies.

A stabled horse that is doing hard work is given a "hunter clip." The hair is clipped from all of its body and neck, except for a patch underneath the saddle.

Safety first!
A horse may get very scared when the clippers are close to its head. If this happens, it is best to leave the head unclipped.

Bathtime

Grooming usually keeps a horse clean, but sometimes—such as before a show—it may need to be bathed with a gentle shampoo. Gray horses and ponies usually have to be bathed more often, but be careful not to overdo it. Too much washing will make a horse's skin and coat dry.

1 Start washing at your horse's neck and work down the front and sides of its body. Wash the mane well too.

Watch what you wear— you may get wet!

Put a halter on your horse so that a helper can hold it.

Your horse will be more comfortable if you use lukewarm water, not cold.

Tail spin
To dry your horse's tail more quickly, swish it around to remove the water.

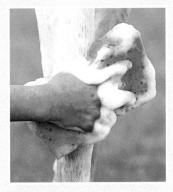

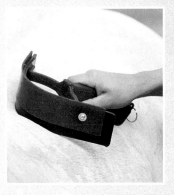

2 Be very gentle when you clean the horse's face. Do not let water and shampoo get into its eyes or ears.

3 Carefully clean the legs. To wash the hind legs, stand at the horse's side, not behind it, in case it tries to kick.

4 Wash the tail by dipping it into a bucket of lukewarm water and then rubbing in shampoo. Rinse it thoroughly.

5 Rinse the horse all over with clean water. Then use a sweat scraper to remove water from its neck and body.

6 Gently comb the mane. Be careful not to break the hairs.

7 Walk the horse around until it is completely dry.

Safety first!
Never give a horse a bath on a cold day because it could get sick.

Outdoor rugs

Have your horse measured to make sure that its blanket fits. It should be snug but not too tight. Check the blanket every day to make sure that it is not causing any sore patches.

The ends of the straps are tucked neatly through the keepers.

The blanket covers the horse's body down to its elbows.

Blankets

Blankets protect horses and ponies from the cold and rain and help keep them clean. There are waterproof blankets for outdoors and stable blankets for horses that live inside. Thermal blankets dry off a sweaty horse, and light summer blankets help keep away flies.

Two straps called surcingles fasten underneath the horse. They keep the blanket in place even if the horse gallops or rolls.

Leg straps are fastened loosely around the horse's hind legs to stop the wind from blowing up the blanket.

The blanket fits snugly around the pony's neck.

Indoor blankets

These are made for stabled horses and are less heavy than outdoor blankets. If your horse is clipped, it will need to wear a blanket for extra warmth, especially at night.

TOP TIP

Clean blanket

Keep your blankets clean by brushing and washing them. Some can go in a washing machine.

front strap

surcingle

Putting on a blanket

1 Place the blanket across your horse's back, far in front of its withers. Do not let the surcingles flap around.

2 Fasten the blanket's surcingles underneath the horse's belly. Be careful not to pull the blanket forward over its coat.

3 Slide the blanket back slightly so that it is snugly in place around the horse's neck. Then fasten the front straps.

4 Lift its tail over the rear strap (fillet string). This helps keep the blanket in place. Speak to your horse to keep it calm.

Bandages

Sometimes a horse's legs need to be bandaged for extra protection—when you are taking it in a trailer to a show or if it has an injury, for example. Bandages should only be put on by an experienced adult.

TOP TIP

Finger test

Slide a finger between the horse's leg and the bandage to check that it is not too tight.

Stable bandages

These are wide bandages that help keep a horse warm in its stable. They must not be too tight.

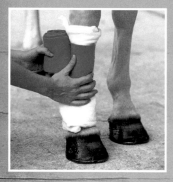

1 The horse's leg is wrapped in a layer of padding. The stable bandage is wound down the leg from just below the knee.

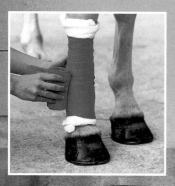

2 With an even pressure, the horse's leg is bandaged down to the fetlock joint and then back up again.

3 The stable bandage is fastened neatly on the outside of the leg, never at the back or the front.

Tail bandages

A tail bandage keeps the hair at the top of a horse's tail flat and neat when it is traveling in a trailer. It also stops the tail from being rubbed. It takes practice to bandage a tail correctly, and an adult should check your work carefully.

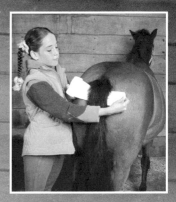

1 Pass the end of the bandage under the dock (the top of your horse's tail).

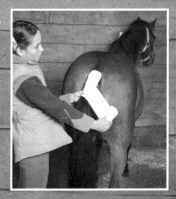

2 Wrap the bandage evenly around and down the horse's tail.

Always tie up your horse when it is being bandaged.

Bandages should be washed often and rolled up tightly so that they are ready to be reused.

3 Finish just above the end of the dock. Tie the tape in a bow, not too tightly.

Bandages are put over a layer of padding— such as gamgee tissue (made from gauze and cotton).

Boots and shoes

When a horse carries a rider, its legs and feet need special care. Boots protect the legs from injuries. Shoes stop the horny part of the hoof from wearing down too quickly and making the horse's feet sore.

body protector

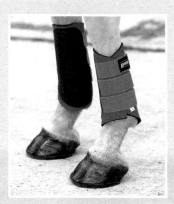

Exercise boots are worn on all four legs. They help prevent injuries, especially if the horse knocks one of its legs against the opposite one.

Tendon boots protect the backs of a horse's forelegs from being hit by the toes of its hind feet. The boots in this picture have an open front.

Overreach boots are worn on the forelegs. They protect the heels of the forelegs from knocks by the toes of the horse's hind feet.

Shoeing a horse

A horse with strong feet that is not doing much work may not need shoes. But most ridden horses wear shoes to protect their feet. The horn of their feet grows all the time, so the shoes must be taken off and the feet trimmed regularly by a farrier.

Safety first!
Check your horse's hooves for cracks. They could be a sign that it has a foot problem.

1 The farrier will probably need to trim your horse's feet every six weeks, but this depends on how fast your horse's feet grow.

2 Shoes are shaped from hot iron, using a hammer and an anvil. Hot shoes fit better than cold ones.

3 The farrier holds the hot shoe on the hoof to check the fit. It does not hurt the horse because the outer part of its foot does not feel anything.

4 The shoe is nailed into place. The farrier takes care not to drive the nails into the sensitive inner part of the foot.

A healthy horse

Horses and ponies are tough animals, but they often get injuries, especially in fields. Try to check your horse or pony every day for cuts, lumps, or skin problems. A good time to do this is when you are grooming it. If you are not sure about anything, ask an adult to call the vet.

The vet will watch your horse trot to see if its shoulders, legs, or feet are injured.

Keep a first-aid box nearby. Inside the box put wound powder, cotton balls, bandages, poultices, sterile dressings, and a pair of curved scissors.

Lameness

This pony is lame, which means that it cannot walk correctly and must not be ridden. The vet is examining the injured leg.

A poultice is a soft pad made from cotton that helps draw dirt or pus from a wound. This foot poultice is kept in place with a bandage.

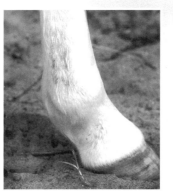

Mud fever is a skin infection that affects horses in very wet weather. Look out for matted hair and scabs around the heels. It must be treated by a vet.

Safety first!

Tetanus is a disease that is caused by germs that live in the soil. To protect your horse from tetanus, it must be given a vaccine, or shot, by a vet.

TOP TIP

Walk out

Sometimes it helps a lame horse to have a short walk every day. Choose a quiet place and always lead it with a bridle.

Cleaning tack

Tack is riding equipment such as saddles, stirrup irons, and bridles. Tack should be cleaned every time it is used. Use a damp sponge to wash off grease and dirt and saddle soap to keep leather soft.

The saddle

Remove the stirrups and girth and clean them separately. Clean the whole saddle, including underneath. Check the stitching and buckles for signs of wear and tear.

stirrup iron

girth

saddle

stirrup leathers

Do not put too much soap on the saddle seat.

Wash any mud off the stirrup irons and dry them with a clean cloth. Metal polish will make them look extra nice.

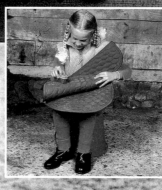

A saddle pad keeps the saddle clean. Brush its underside after every use and wash it often with mild detergent.

The bridle

After every ride, clean and then dry
the bit. The best way to clean the whole
bridle is to take it apart.

1 With a damp sponge, clean
off all of the grease and dirt.
Do not wet the leather—this
will make it hard.

browband

noseband

throatlatch

bit

reins

2 Rub a small amount of
saddle soap into all of the
straps. From time to time, use
a special leather conditioner.

3 Put the bridle back
together. Fasten all of
the buckles and studs and
push the ends of the straps
through the keepers.

Tacked up

It is important that your horse's tack fits correctly. The bit must be the right size for its mouth. The straps of the bridle must be carefully adjusted to fit your horse's head comfortably. All horses and ponies are different shapes, so it is best if each one has its own saddle.

The pommel of the saddle must not press on the horse's withers (the bump at the base of its neck).

A well-padded saddle will not hurt your horse's backbone.

The girth should hold the saddle firmly in place without pinching your horse's skin.

Safety first!
Before you mount, check that the girth is tight enough to stop the saddle from slipping.

Lead-rein riding

The safest way to begin riding is on a lead line. The leader walks or jogs beside the horse, keeping it under control, while you learn how to sit in the saddle and how to hold and use the reins. The leader should be an older, experienced person.

Learning to trot is best done on the lead line. To begin with, you may need to hold the front of the saddle. Never pull on the reins to stay balanced.

The noseband sits well above the horse's nostrils.

The throatlatch must not be too tight.

The stirrup iron is attached to the saddle by a leather strap. This safety iron has an elastic side that allows your foot to slide out if you fall off.

TOP TIP

Lunging

Sending a horse around in circles on the end of a long rein is called lunging. Riding on the lunge without reins will help you learn to balance in the saddle.

Ready to go out

Before you go out for a ride, check that your tack is in good condition. Always wear the correct riding clothes. If you are going on the road, you must make sure that other road users can see you clearly.

Stirrups are the right length when your finger is on the stirrup leather buckle and the bottom of the iron reaches your armpit.

In cold weather, your horse may need to wear an exercise sheet. Choose one with reflective strips.

When you are in the saddle, you may need to tighten the girth by one more hole.

Brushing boots stop your horse from knocking its foot against the inside of the opposite leg.

42

A correctly fitted helmet is the most important piece of riding equipment.

Wear a vest with reflective strips on the front and back.

Phone home
Take a cell phone with you so that you can call for help if you have a problem.

Wear gloves to give you a better grip on the reins.

Always check that your tack is correctly fitted before you go out. Never use a bridle or a saddle with worn stitching.

Always wear the correct riding boots, never sneakers.

Warming up and down
Do not start trotting or cantering as soon as you set off. First, walk your horse for a while to loosen up its muscles. When you go home, especially after a fast ride, always walk the last mile or two. Your horse should be cool and not out of breath when it reaches its stable.

To turn left or right, hold your arm out straight, with a flat palm facing the front.

To ask a car in front of you to stop, raise your hand, with the palm facing forward.

To ask a car behind you to drive past, move your hand in a forward movement, with your arm straight.

TOP TIP

Thank you

After you make a signal, look at the driver and say thank you by smiling and nodding your head.

Riding safely

Ride on roads only if your horse or pony is not scared of traffic. Stay alert at all times because something other than a vehicle might scare your horse. You need to learn how to make signals to other road users. Practice these at home.

Hold both reins (and your whip if you have one) in one hand.

Make sure that you open the gate far enough for the horse to walk through without hitting itself against the post.

Gates

Being able to open and shut a gate without dismounting is very useful when you go for a ride in the countryside. Practice riding the horse around the gate and through the gap. Most horses will quickly learn how to do this.

Always close the gate securely behind you to stop any farm animals from getting out of their fields.

Galloping

One of the most exciting things you can do with your horse or pony is to go for a gallop. You must be a good, confident rider.

Fast riding

Remember that horses and ponies love to gallop too. They can become very excited, especially when they are heading home! Make sure that the owners of the land do not mind if you gallop your horse or pony in their field.

TOP TIP

Hometime

If you walk the last mile back to the stable, your horse will arrive home cool and relaxed. Groom it and then put on its blanket before you feed it.

Safety first!
If you gallop with other riders, leave plenty of room between each horse.

Glossary

Boarding barn
You pay someone to keep your horse at a boarding barn. It will cost less if you do some of the work yourself such as mucking out.

Breed
A horse or pony group that has been bred carefully over a period of time.

Colic
This is a stomach pain, often caused by eating too much or by a sudden change in diet. A horse that has colic may sweat and repeatedly roll on the ground.

Currycomb
A grooming tool made out of metal, rubber, or plastic. A metal currycomb is used to clean the body brush. A rubber or plastic currycomb is used to remove mud from the horse's coat.

Farrier
A person who trims a horse's feet and makes and fits its shoes. Another word for a farrier is a blacksmith.

Hands
Traditionally, horses and ponies are measured in hands. One hand equals 4 in. (10cm), which is around the width of an adult's hand.

Horn
The wall of a horse's hoof is made out of horn, which, like our fingernails, keeps on growing and does not feel pain when it is trimmed.

Horse pellets
A type of feed that has been ground up, steamed, and then shaped into small pellets.

Lame
When a horse has hurt its foot or leg and cannot walk correctly.

Laminitis
If a horse eats too much rich food or doesn't exercise enough, the inside parts of its hooves can swell up. This is known as laminitis.

Sweet feed
A concentrated feed of whole or crushed grains (oats, barley, and corn, for example) mixed with molasses to make it sweet for the horse.

Thrush
This foot infection is usually caused by standing in wet bedding. The horse's foot begins to rot and smells bad.

Vet (short for veterinarian)
A highly trained person who looks after the health of animals.

Withers
The top of a horse's shoulders, between the neck and the back.

Worms
These harmful parasites live inside horses and ponies. To control the problem, you need to treat your horse or pony with special powders or pastes.

Index

Acknowledgements

The publisher would like to thank the following for their help in the production of this book:

Models: Alexis, Amy, Charley, Charlotte, Ciara, Elliot, Fraser, Harry, Hollie, India, Justice, Leanne, Lucy, Raija, Rhianna and Simi

Ponies: Cracker, Denzel, Jasper, Pickwick, Pie, Rosie, Scamp, Big Scamp, Teddy and Tiger

Lisa Benton and Pat Seager

The Justine Armstrong-Small team (www.armstrong-small.co.uk): Justine and Hazel Armstrong-Small

Grooms: Becky, Katie, Lisa and Vicky

Jason Robertson, registered farrier

Harolds Park Farm Riding Centre

Cuddly Ponies, Dublin Clothing and Roma (www.dublinclothing.com)

Photography: Matthew Roberts (www.matthewrobertsphotographer.com)

All photographs by Matthew Roberts with the exception of: page 8cl, 14bl, 15cr, 15br, 37tr (Bob Langrish, www.boblangrish.co.uk), 8bl (Shutterstock/Jaco Wiid), 9bl (Shutterstock/Rita Kochmarjova), Cover (KuznetsovDmitry/iStock Images)